Amazing Animals
Monkeys

Please visit our web site at www.garethstevens.com
For a free catalog describing our list of high-quality books, call 1-800-542-2595 (USA) or 1-800-387-3178 (Canada).
Our fax: 1-877-542-2596

Library of Congress Cataloging-in-Publication Data

Wilsdon, Christina.
    Monkeys / by Christina Wilsdon.—U.S. ed.
          p. cm.—(Amazing Animals)
      Includes bibliographical references and index.
      Originally published: Pleasantville, NY : Reader's Digest Young Families, c2007.
      ISBN-10: 0-8368-9109-0 ISBN-13: 978-0-8368-9109-6 (lib. bdg.)
      ISBN-10: 1-4339-2026-3 ISBN-13: 978-1-4339-2026-4 (soft cover)
    1. Monkeys—Juvenile literature. I. Title.
    QL737.P9W634 2009
    599.8—dc22   2008027904

This edition first published in 2009 by
Gareth Stevens Publishing
A Weekly Reader® Company
1 Reader's Digest Road
Pleasantville, NY 10570-7000 USA

This edition copyright © 2009 by Gareth Stevens, Inc. Original edition copyright © 2007 by Reader's Digest Young Families,
Pleasantville, NY 10570

Gareth Stevens Senior Managing Editor: Lisa M. Herrington
Gareth Stevens Creative Director: Lisa Donovan
Gareth Stevens Art Director: Ken Crossland
Gareth Stevens Associate Editor: Amanda Hudson
Gareth Stevens Publisher: Keith Garton

Consultant: Robert E. Budliger (Retired), NY State Department of Environmental Conservation

Photo Credits
Front cover: Stanislav Khrapov/Shutterstock Inc., Title page: Dynamic Graphics Inc., Contents: Nova Development Corporation, pages 6-7:
Simone van den Berg/Shutterstock Inc., page 8: Eric Gevaert/Shutterstock Inc., pages 11-12: Simone van den Berg/Shutterstock Inc., pages
14-15: Dynamic Graphics Inc., page 16: Ra'id Khalil/Shutterstock Inc., page 19: Dynamic Graphics Inc., page 21: Steffen Foerster Photography/
Shutterstock Inc., pages 22-23: Brand X Pictures, page 24: Jupiter Images, pages 25 and 26: Corel Corporation, pages 27-28: Brand X Pictures,
page 29: Dynamic Graphics Inc., pages 30-31: Stanislav Khrapov/Shutterstock Inc., page 32: Chris Bence/Shutterstock Inc., page 33: Dreamstime.
com/Steffen Foerster, page 35: Jiri Cvrk/Shutterstock Inc., page 36: Dynamic Graphics Inc., pages 38-39: WizData, Inc./Shutterstock Inc., page
41: Steffen Foerster/Shutterstock Inc., page 43: Photodisc/Getty Images, pages 44-45: Image 100 Ltd., Back cover: Steffen Foerster Photography/
Shutterstock Inc.

Every effort has been made to trace the copyright holders for the photos used in this book, and the publisher apologizes in advance for any
unintentional omissions. We would be pleased to insert the appropriate acknowledgements in any subsequent edition of this publication.

Printed in the United States of America

1 2 3 4 5 6 7 8 9 13 12 11 10 09

Amazing Animals
Monkeys

By Christina Wilsdon

Gareth Stevens
Publishing

Contents

A Monkey Story

The mother monkey climbed up onto a branch. Parrots screeched in the treetops above. Monkeys squeaked on the branches below. But the noise did not bother the baby monkey. He was fast asleep on his mother's back.

The baby monkey was just a few days old. He spent most of his time draped across his mother, gripping her fur with his fingers. Sometimes the mother monkey cuddled him in her arms as he drank the milk that her body made for him.

The mother and baby lived in a rain forest. They were part of a big group of squirrel monkeys. The monkeys scampered through the trees during the day, searching for insects and fruit.

The mother needed to look carefully to find food. She also had to keep her eyes open for danger. There were many animals in the rain forest that might eat a little monkey. She checked the skies to watch out for eagles. She checked the branches to make sure no snakes were sneaking up on her.

If the mother monkey saw danger, she made loud noises that sounded like "*chuck-chuck-chuck*" to warn the other monkeys.

When the baby monkey was about five weeks old, he was ready to explore. He spent less time on his mother's back and more time swinging through the branches. Sometimes leaves blocked his view of his mother, but he could always hear her call or smell her scent. If he cried out, his mother would quickly appear and scoop him into her arms.

The baby monkey watched his mother and the other adult monkeys when they found food. Soon he began trying these foods, too. He tasted new leaves and sweet fruits. He sipped nectar from flowers and chomped on nuts. Sometimes he snacked on snails and tree frogs. Once he even found a nest full of eggs.

But best of all were the tasty insects that clung to leaves. The baby monkey learned that curled-up leaves often held hidden caterpillars. For a monkey, unfolding these leaves was like opening a candy bar!

The Color of Fruit

Squirrel monkeys can see in color. This helps them find ripe fruits among the green leaves.

High, But Not Highest

Squirrel monkeys live in the middle levels of the treetops, not at the very top where spider monkeys live.

The baby monkey grew bigger and stronger. He learned how to run along a branch without falling off. Soon he was jumping from branch to branch. He used his long tail to help him balance. He chased other baby monkeys through the trees.

Sometimes the squirrel monkeys followed groups of other kinds of monkeys. The groups did not work together to find food. But they did share the same trees. By following other kinds of monkeys, the squirrel monkeys found fruit that they may not have found on their own.

Being part of a larger group helped all the monkeys. With more eyes and ears on the alert for danger, it was harder for a **predator** to catch a monkey.

By the time the baby monkey was a year old, his mother was busy taking care of his newborn baby sister! But the baby monkey would not be fully grown until he was about four years old. Until then, he would spend his time with other young male monkeys, playing and swinging in the treetops.

Chapter 2
The Body of a Monkey

Monkeys Are Primates

Monkeys are part of a group of animals called **primates**. Primates have large brains, thumbs that are opposite the other four "fingers," and eyes at the front of their faces. Chimpanzees, apes, and humans are primates, too.

Seeing Red

Monkeys see in much the same way that you do. Their eyes are at the front of their heads, like yours. This helps them see how close or far away something is. The ability is very important when leaping from branch to branch! The position of the eyes also lets monkeys see and identify what is in their hands.

Most monkeys see in color. Monkeys from Africa and Asia see in full color. But some monkeys from Mexico, Central America, and South America cannot see red or reddish colors, such as orange. Seeing red helps monkeys pick out ripe fruit among the thick green leaves. No one is sure why some kinds of monkeys do not see in full color.

Hearing and Smelling

Monkeys do not hear the same wide range of sounds that humans do. But their sense of smell is much better than ours. Monkeys use smells to help them pick ripe fruit. Many monkeys use smells to **communicate** with other monkeys. The squirrel monkey leaves scent trails on branches with its hands and feet.

Monkeys that cannot see red colors seem to have a sharper sense of smell than monkeys with full-color vision. This may make up for not being able to see well in color.

Hands and Feet

Like humans, most monkeys have a thumb and four other "fingers" on each hand. This arrangement lets monkeys grip branches and pick up things by pinching them between their thumb and fingers.

A monkey's foot has five toes, like a human's foot. But a monkey's toes are very long and can wrap around branches. The toes are arranged in a way that helps them grip. The big toe on the inside of the foot is shorter than the others and works more like a thumb. A monkey seems to have four hands instead of two!

Nails and Claws

Most monkeys have flat nails on their fingers and toes, just as humans do. Nails make it easier to grip things. Claws would get in the way.

Having flat nails also lets monkeys feel things more easily with their fingertips. The fingertips have bumpy patterns called fingerprints, which improve a monkey's grip. A monkey's fingerprints are unique, just as yours are!

Unlike most monkeys, the tiny monkeys called marmosets have claws on most of their fingers and toes. Only their big toes have nails. Claws help marmosets climb up tree trunks.

A monkey can use its fingers to pluck a pesky insect from fur or a single berry from a bush.

Thumbs Down

A few kinds of monkeys do not have thumbs. The colobus monkey has just a tiny bump instead of a thumb. It grasps branches by using its fingers as hooks.

Getting Around

How a monkey gets around depends on where it lives. Monkeys that live in trees have powerful hind legs for jumping from branch to branch and tree to tree.

A few kinds of monkeys use their arms to swing through the trees, holding on with just their hands. A black spider monkey moves this way. It has extra-long arms and long fingers that hook over branches.

Monkeys that live on the ground have long arms and strong muscles in their shoulders. This helps them move on all four feet and run from danger.

Monkey Tails

All monkeys have tails. Tails help monkeys keep their balance. Some have very long tails, like the black spider monkey. The shortest tail belongs to the Barbary macaque.

A tail that can be used to grasp objects is called a **prehensile** (pre HEN sill) **tail**. Spider monkeys, woolly monkeys, and howler monkeys all have prehensile tails. These monkeys hang onto branches with their long tails. They pick fruit and leaves with their hands.

Monkeys that live in trees are super jumpers! But most of them can't hang by their tails. Only monkeys that live in Mexico, Central America, and South America can hang by their tails.

Pad Prints

A monkey that can hang by its tail has a bare patch of skin on the bottom side of the tip of its tail. The bare patch is called a **friction pad**. The pad is lined with ridges that help the tail grip branches without slipping. Each monkey's "friction-pad print" is unique, just as your fingerprints are.

22

Chapter 3
Kinds of Monkeys

The mandrill lives in Africa and is an Old World monkey. It is closely related to the baboon, which is the biggest type of monkey.

Old World Monkeys

Monkeys are divided into two main groups—**Old World monkeys** and **New World monkeys**.

Old World monkeys live in Africa and Asia. Their noses are not as wide as the noses of New World monkeys. Their nostrils point downward, like yours do, and are usually curved.

Most Old World monkeys have fingers and thumbs that are better at gripping than those of New World monkeys.

Old World monkeys have tough, bare patches on their hind ends. The patches make it more comfortable to sit on branches.

New World Monkeys

New World monkeys live in Mexico, Central America, and South America. Their nostrils are usually round and point outward instead of down.

Cotton-top tamarin

New World monkeys do not have bare patches on their hind ends. Their tails are longer than the tails of Old World monkeys. Some New World monkeys can hang by their tails, but no Old World monkeys can. All New World monkeys live in trees.

Snow Monkey

"Snow monkey" is a nickname for an Old World monkey called the Japanese macaque. This monkey lives farther north than any other kind of monkey.

Japanese macaques are famous for learning new ways of doing things and passing them on to other monkeys. One macaque figured out how to separate grains of wheat from sand. She threw the mixture into water, let the sand sink, and then ate the grains that floated to the top. The rest of her **troop** copied her. Monkey see, monkey do!

Macaques that live near hot springs keep warm by soaking in the warm water. They get out of these "hot tubs" and dry off before going up into trees to sleep.

Ground Monkey

The patas monkey is an Old World monkey found in Africa. It lives on the ground in dry, grassy lands called **savannas**. It has long legs that help it run fast—about 30 miles (48 km) an hour! At night, it climbs up into a tree to sleep, where it is out of the reach of many predators.

Patas monkey

In winter, Japanese macaques grow thick coats of fur that help keep them warm.

Scientists think the red face of a bald uakari is a sign of good health. A female uakari is more likely to pick a healthy, red-faced male for a mate than a pale-faced male that might be sick.

Bald Monkey

Bald uakaris are New World monkeys with bald, red heads and short tails. They are also called red uakaris. Some bald uakaris have white fur. Others have rusty-red fur. A baby bald uakari is not bald. Its head is covered with gray hair. It goes bald by the time it is an adult.

Bald uakaris live in swampy areas of rain forests. They usually live in troops of up to 30 monkeys.

Pygmy marmoset

Mini Monkey

The world's smallest monkey is a New World monkey called the pygmy marmoset. Its body is just 5 inches (13 centimeters) long—about the length of a dollar bill!

Pygmy marmosets move through the trees like squirrels. A marmoset uses its teeth to dig holes in tree trunks. The monkey then eats the sap that oozes from these holes. A marmoset collects food from its "farm" of tree holes like a farmer gathers sap from maple trees.

30

Chapter 4
A Monkey's Life

Most monkeys prefer to eat tender, new leaves or just the tips of leaves. They are softer and easier to digest than fully grown leaves.

To-Go Meals

Some kinds of Old World monkeys have cheek pouches for carrying food. The monkeys stuff food into the pouches, then go to a safe spot to chew and swallow it.

Monkey Meals

Monkeys eat both plants and other animals. Scientists call these animals **omnivores** (OM nih vorz).

The favorite food of monkeys is fruit. New World monkeys eat more than 70 kinds of fruit.

Monkeys also eat seeds, nuts, sap, and bark. Bearded saki monkeys use their strong teeth to open Brazil nuts. These nuts have shells that are so tough that humans often boil them before trying to open them!

Insects, spiders, birds' eggs, lizards, and baby birds are also on most monkey menus. Big African monkeys called baboons catch and eat young gazelles. Mangabeys of Africa sometimes eat snakes. Long-tailed macaques of Southeast Asia eat crabs, shrimp, and even octopus!

Banana Peels

Monkeys are famous for eating bananas—and for peeling them from the bottom up. Humans peel bananas from the stem down.

Monkey Talk

Monkeys use different sounds to talk with each other. Many monkeys use peeps and squeaks to "chat" with friends or baby monkeys.

Louder noises are used when monkeys are far apart or can't see each other in the treetops. These sounds help a troop stay together. Sometimes sounds alert family members to a patch of ripe fruit.

Many monkeys use loud sounds to warn of danger. These sounds give clear information about what kind of danger is near. Some monkeys make loud noises to warn other groups of monkeys away from their territory.

Body Language

Monkeys use their faces and bodies to send messages. A monkey may threaten another monkey by opening its mouth wide and showing its teeth. Staring and slapping the ground are signs of anger. A male mandrill shoves his colorful face at another mandrill and pokes out his lips while the hair on his head rises up!

Monkeys use sounds and body language to talk with each other.

Monkey Code

When a monkey calls out, other monkeys know exactly what the sound means. A vervet monkey barks when it sees a leopard. This makes other monkeys hide in trees. If it sees an eagle, it coughs in a way that makes other monkeys look up. If it sees a snake, it makes a chattering sound that causes other monkeys to look down at the grass.

Monkeys spend a lot of time grooming each other. Grooming keeps fur clean. Grooming also helps monkeys feel friendly and calm toward each other and keeps bonds between group members strong.

Monkey Groups

All monkeys live in groups. Some kinds of monkeys live in a small family group that has a male, a female, and a baby or two. Other kinds of monkeys live in larger groups.

Still other kinds of monkeys live in groups that have only one male monkey. He is the leader. He is often challenged by other males. If he loses a fight, a new male takes over.

Baby Monkeys

Most monkeys have just one baby at a time. Some have twins or triplets.

Baby monkeys stay with their mothers for the first few weeks of life. Some kinds of babies hang from the bellies of their mothers. Others cling to their mothers' backs. A few kinds of monkey moms give the babies to their mates to carry. A male titi monkey carries his babies all the time. He only gives them back to their mom for a quick drink of milk!

Baby monkeys may look different from their parents. A baby silvered langur is bright orange. A baby black-and-white colobus monkey has fuzzy white fur. Scientists think these differences help make adult monkeys more patient with babies. The colors signal, "I'm just a baby!"

38

Chapter 5
Monkeys in the World

Where Monkeys Live

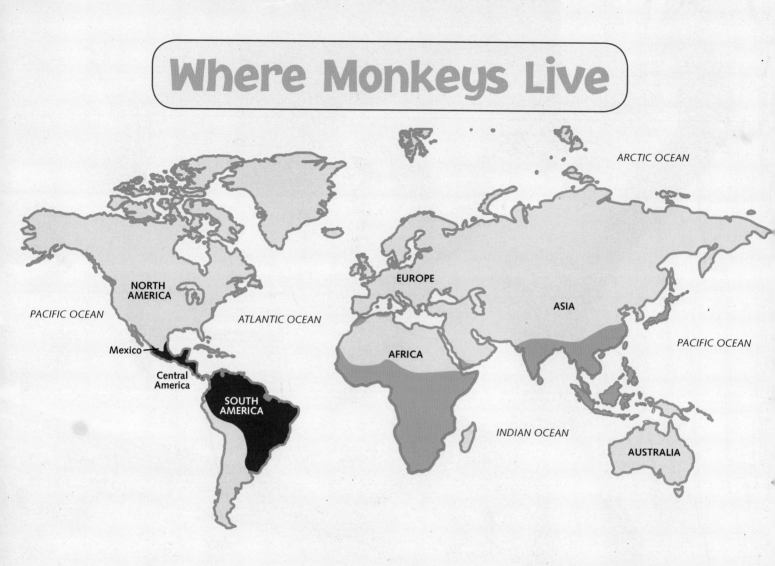

ARCTIC OCEAN

NORTH
AMERICA

PACIFIC OCEAN

ATLANTIC OCEAN

EUROPE

ASIA

PACIFIC OCEAN

Mexico

AFRICA

Central
America

SOUTH
AMERICA

INDIAN OCEAN

AUSTRALIA

The **purple** areas show where New World monkeys live.

The green areas show where Old World monkeys live.

Threats to Monkeys

Monkeys face many threats to their survival. The biggest threat is the loss of their **habitats**. Many kinds of monkeys live in tropical forests that are being cut down for lumber or burned to clear space for farms and ranch lands. Without forests, monkeys and other animals have no place to live.

Hunting is also a threat. Some kinds of monkeys are killed for their fur as well as their meat. In some places, people have killed so many monkeys that there are now very few left.

Sacred Monkeys

In some places, monkeys are considered **sacred**. In India and Sri Lanka, the Hanuman langur is named after Hanuman, the Hindu god of monkeys, whose face, hands, and feet were blackened by fire as he rescued a queen. Hanuman langurs have black faces, hands, and feet. Today, these sacred monkeys are allowed to roam freely and are often found in or near temples.

Hanuman langurs

The Future of Monkeys

Many countries have passed laws that protect monkeys and help to control their capture and sale. In 1975, the United States passed a law making it **illegal** to bring monkeys into the country to sell them as pets. These laws have not ended threats to monkeys, but they are steps in the right direction.

Monkeys are also helped by people working to save habitats. Tropical forests that are set aside as parks and preserves provide homes for monkeys and other animals.

Some zoos are working with the governments of different countries to help endangered monkeys. In recent years, the government of Brazil has worked with zoos and scientists to save the golden lion tamarin that lives in the rain forest.

Fast Facts About Squirrel Monkeys

Scientific name	*Saimiri sciureus*
Class	Mammalia
Order	Primates
Weight	2 to 3 pounds (1 kilogram)
Life span	Up to 20 years
Habitat	Tropical rain forests

42

In the 1970s, fewer than 200 golden lion tamarins lived in the wild. Today there are about 1,500 golden lion tamarins in the protected rain forests of Brazil.

Glossary

communicate — to exchange thoughts, feelings, and information through sounds, facial expressions, and behavior

friction pad — a bare patch of skin on the underside of some monkeys' tails

groom — to clean fur, skin, or feathers

habitat — the natural environment where an animal or plant lives

illegal — against the laws of a place

New World monkeys — the monkeys of Mexico, Central America, and South America

Old World monkeys — the monkeys of Asia and Africa

44

omnivore — an animal that eats both plants and other animals

predator — an animal that hunts and eats other animals to survive

prehensile tail — a tail that can grip and hold on to objects

primates — a group of mammals with large brains and thumbs that are opposite the other four fingers. Monkeys, chimpanzees, and humans are primates.

sacred — holy

savanna — a flat grassland area with scattered trees in a hot region of the world

troop — a group of monkeys

tropical — relating to hot and humid places

Monkeys: Show What You Know

How much have you learned about monkeys? Grab a piece of paper and a pencil and write your answers down.

1. Why do most monkeys have flat nails instead of claws on their fingers and toes?

2. What is the name for the kind of tail that can be used to grasp objects?

3. Which type of monkey has the shortest tail?

4. What is the name of the bare patch of skin on the tail of a monkey who hangs from trees?

5. What are the two main groups that monkeys are divided into?

6. Which type of monkey is the largest?

7. On which continents do Old World monkeys live?

8. "Snow monkey" is the nickname for which type of monkey?

9. Which type of monkey is the smallest?

10. What is the biggest threat to the survival of monkeys?

1. Because nails make it easier to grab things 2. Prehensile tail 3. The Barbary macaque 4. Friction pad 5. Old World monkeys and New World monkeys 6. The baboon 7. Africa and Asia 8. Japanese macaque 9. The pygmy marmoset 10. The loss of their habitats

For More Information

Books

Apes and Monkeys. Science Kids (series). Taylor, Barbara. (Kingfisher, 2007)

Gorilla, Monkey & Ape. Eyewitness Books (series). Redmond, Ian.
(DK Children, 2000)

Monkeys. Our Wild World (series). Dennard, Deborah. (NorthWord Books, 2003)

Web Sites

National Geographic Kids: Howler Monkeys

www.kids.nationalgeographic.com/Animals/CreatureFeature/Howler-monkey

Learn all about the amazing howler monkey and its loud call. Be sure to check out
the video clips to hear it for yourself!

San Diego Zoo: Monkeys

www.sandiegozoo.org/animalbytes/t-monkey.html

Check out this site for monkey facts, photos, and information about the Endangered
Primate Rescue Center.

Publisher's note to educators and parents: Our editors have carefully reviewed these web sites
to ensure that they are suitable for children. Many web sites change frequently, however, and we
cannot guarantee that a site's future contents will continue to meet our high standards of quality and
educational value. Be advised that children should be closely supervised whenever they access the Internet.

Index